CULTURAL DNA

DISCOVERING AND UNCOVERING

Nicole Yan

Dedication

To my mother, God's strongest soldier.

To Terrence Mooney. I hope you're okay with me using your first name.

Acknowledgements

My first debt is to Emma and Kristina, my guiding counselor and writing mentor in this publishing process. I would not have been able to get this work done without your continuous support, considerate support and tremendous efforts behind the scenes. Thank you so much for countless hours reviewing my work from notes to excerpts to drafts. You made this possible. Thank you so much again.

To Alice, for pushing me to bring this story out to more people. It would have been impossible for me to have found my own identity without you.

To my mother, my daily inspiration and my hero. Thank you for being with me through all the highs and the lows. I am forever inspired by your strength and I'm glad to say that I found it inside of me, too. Thank you so much for everything.

And to Mr. Mooney, thank you for redirecting my writing from a place of rage and cynicism to a place of love. I would not be able to write the way I do without your guidance. I'm proud to say that, for a moment, I found my voice as a writer.

Book Proceeds Donation

The profit from this book will be donated to The Yan AAPI Well-being Fund - which seeks to build a safer, more inclusive world for all aspects of the AAPI community. The AAPI community, especially those of other minority groups, such as the LGBTQ+ community, suffers from alarming rates of mental health challenges and suicide attempts. In addition, these youths face a similar yet unique set of challenges to the overall immigrant and LGBTQ+ community, such as the combination of anti-LGBTQ+ victimization and immigration-based discrimination.

This fund hopes to donate and fundraise for non-profit organizations that support all Asian American and Pacific Islander communities through crisis services, peer support, research, public education, and advocacy.

CONTENTS

Chapter I

Childhood

My Name

My American name is Nicole. Well, before that it was Nickhole, and before that it was Nikholas. When I was six, my mama decided I needed an American name because none of my teachers seem to be able to say Hongyi without sounding like a honking goose. And so she took it upon herself to give me something more "fitting" for America.

As someone who chose my given name with such rigor, it often surprises me how carelessly she landed on Nicole. The name itself means something like "victory of the people," but as far as I'm concerned, I'm pretty sure my mom just took the first name she could find on television. Yet this name, chosen with such little care, has stuck with me my entire life.

I tend to think of names as these stupid invisible forcefields of connotations. And for that reason, I've never appreciated my name. Nicole is associated with suburban whiteness. Nicole is a perfect housewife who bakes cookies on Sundays for church. Nicole is a girl not girly enough to be popular but also not tomboyish enough to be a cool cat. Nicole was the last person I wanted to be.

Yet I stuck with Nicole. I stuck with it because Hongyi got lost in pronunciation as people try to cough up the second syllable. I stuck with it because I didn't want to spell out h-o-n-g-y-i every time a school counselor asked for my name. I stuck with it because part of me would rather be a suburban, average white girl than Chinese like the two characters that made up my given name.

And so, for the next six years, I would try on more names than I do clothes: Vivian, Victoria, Cole, Nick, Isabelle, Isa, Bella. Every name felt like part of me but not entirely. They were all versions and connotations of who I wanted to be.

And for right now, all my friends call me Kat, short for Katarina. I think that maybe someday, one day, eventually in the future, I would like to change my legal name to Katarina.

Color

What's your favorite color? That's always my go-to question. Something about colors fascinates me. Red seems passionate, blue seems versatile, green seems calm, yellow seems exuberant, purple seems mysterious. So many connotations associated with something as simple as colors.

I think a person's favorite color says a lot about them. In one word, I have an image of how they deal with life. I have a general idea of who they are. Maybe that's why my favorite color changes all the time – because I can't decide on what kind of person I want to be. When I was younger, my favorite color was blue growing up. And then it was black. Until, of course, I realized that black isn't a color. Sometime more recently, I decided my favorite color was red. Not because I like wearing it or that it's beautiful. Just because I like all the things associated with red. I think red is a very bold color. I like the idea of approaching life being bold.

While I can't decide what my favorite color is, I know that my least favorite color has always been gray. Gray is a muddied mix of everything. Not red enough to be red, not blue enough to be blue, not yellow enough to be yellow. Gray is terrible in how it can't seem to decide what it wants to be. Gray seems insecure to me. Insecure and indecisive. That's why I hate gray. Moderation. In between. Never good enough. Gray.

Eyes

Everybody on my dad's side of the family has the same eyes. The same small, brown, squinting eyes that remind people of beady little mice that steal grain from farmers. Every time I hear someone say that *eyes are the windows to the soul,* I cringe. Windows to what soul? And while I understand that in Chinese culture, eyes like ours represent descendancy from the phoenix, to me, they represent permanent rage and unrest. Eyes like ours are windows to tired souls.

Eyes on my mama's side of the family are a different story. My mama has the prettiest doe eyes I've ever seen. Her eyes light up at every story that she tells, lights up every time she holds you and kisses your forehead. Her eyes remind everyone who looks into them of autumn and honey, of freshly baked cinnamon rolls, and of springtime sunshine that warms your body as you lounge away mornings in bed with a cup of freshly brewed oolong tea. I wish I had my mother's eyes.

Aunt Nenny

My Aunt Nenny got a divorce with her husband when I was four because they were "not compatible." I don't really know if I believe her because if incompatibility is what breaks couples up, then none of my friends' parents should still be together. But still, I gladly took the love that she had to spare and bathed in it.

Aunt Nenny is basically my second mama, or "Auntma" as I like to call it. Her love for me was unconditional. She took care of me every single day like my cousin didn't exist. She took care of me like he didn't live right down the block. She took care of me like I was her daughter. I never brought him up because every time I did, she would just shake her head and curse. Regardless, Aunt Nenny and I were best friends. She slept with me during the nights my mama was out on a business trip. She cooked, she cleaned, and she danced. She taught me how to sway my hips and sing lullabies. We hiked over every mountain in our 10-mile radius and we planted our own little garden. I loved Aunt Nenny. And at the prime age of six, love meant fun and games and a good pot of porridge.

As I grew up, I pieced together Aunt Nenny's story from my other relatives. I learned that she got married at 19 after she dropped out of college for my dad's tuition. As far as I know, it was an arranged marriage that my granny set up to optimize the money earned by selling out her eldest daughter. I always wondered if Aunt Nenny regretted that decision, and it wasn't until way too recently that I finally got my answer.

I saw Aunt Nenny's ex-husband over winter break when he swung around to the family mansion. Money, he croaked, Money, and stuck out his hand like he owned the place. Everywhere he walked he left the stench of alcohol and women. Greed clung to every crease of his shirt. When he laughed, he bared his yellow teeth, and every time he raised the bottle in his right hand, I could see Aunt Nenny visibly wince. His beard stuck out in every direction and although his homeless disposition looked nothing like my well-organized, stern cousin, I could see a shadow of him in my cousin's slender figure. I finally understood why Aunt Nenny pretends like my cousin doesn't exist.

People say that my Aunt Nenny got lucky. They say she got lucky because she was able to get out of that marriage. That she got lucky because the brother she gave up her education for was able to bring the family out of the starving rural towns. She got lucky because he gave her a place in his house when the only place a divorced woman with a high school education should've ended up was the streets. They say that she got lucky to be my Auntma. That she got lucky because I loved her despite her being a scrubby, beat-up woman. She got lucky because I will defend her no matter what and because I'm the only reason she has a place to stay.

But I don't think Aunt Nenny got very lucky at all. I didn't fall in love with her for no reason. I loved her because she gave me love in a household where love ran thin. I loved her because she loved me when nobody else in my family would. I loved her because neither of my parents wanted me when she did. I don't care if people say her love is parasitical. I don't care if I was just an accidental safe place she found to store all the love she wanted to give my cousin but couldn't. I don't care that she clings to this love so hard it breaks my bones. I'm so so tired of being the sole reason she wants to live. But I don't care. I promised my six-year-old self that I would always love her unconditionally.

Fat Lady

Fat, I said, pointing straight at my nursery teacher. The 22nd English word I'd learned. My mom always told me to try and put new words to use. And in the matter of seconds, I witnessed just how fast red could inch up someone's face as she plumed up in anger. She took three huge breaths in before she tried to talk.

You did NOT just say that to me, she hollered.

Fat, I repeated.

The result of that short dialogue was me becoming the first ever kid in the nursery to end up in what was the equivalent of detention. As I sat alone in the dark room, I found myself staring at the only light coming from the crack of the door. I felt lost. I had no idea why my nursery teacher was mad at all. I mean, it was like saying a fire hydrant was red. There was no bad intention, no attack, and not even a second thought in that statement. Just a description that I had learned that day in the coloring book.

I think when we grow up words get too clouded with all these connotations and social prejudices and experiences we want to forget. But for a kid at the age of five, there was nothing to the word "fat." No hate, no judgment. Just another word in the dictionary. I guess I didn't feel like I deserved to be sitting in this room because I cried. I know I cried because I remember my mama complaining about my soaked shirt when I came home. I guess sometimes words should be held back. Maybe it's easier to keep my mouth shut.

Queen Valerie and Her Watery Eyes

Use your words, people say.

Speak up, people say.

Talk louder, people say.

But I'm not good at speaking up or using my words or talking loud because I don't really want to be heard. It's not like people try to understand anyway. They just tell you you're making excuses and end up believing Queen Valerie every time.

I met Valerie in third grade. She was mean and she was loud and she used her words. She used to dominate our little playground and she made people listen to her. Everyone was forced to roleplay as her pet cat or dog or servant while she pretended to be a little princess who liked pink.

All hail Queen Valerie, we would say.

Bow down to Queen Valerie, we would repeat.

And so we did. Our knees bent and heads lowered and we learned to be her little playthings. No one chose whether they wanted to be friends with Queen Valerie. Queen Valerie chose them. I know this because when I told the other kids I didn't want to be friends with a mean girl, I got locked up in detention by my homeroom teacher for bullying. There was nothing Queen Valerie couldn't get by batting her huge watery eyes and pouting her little pink lips. The school knew nothing about her.

After the third time I tried to get a group rebellion going, I was sent to the principal in the middle of history class by my homeroom teacher.

If you keep up the bullying you'll be suspended, Ms. Carter said.

I didn't bully anyone, I said in defense.

Well for your information, young lady, spreading false rumors about someone is bullying. And don't you dare lie to me again because I can see it in your eyes that you're not sorry, she replied.

I'm not, I told her. Plus, it's only a rumor if it's false.

Miss Yan, this is not up for debate. If you don't stop squinting your eyes and catching an attitude with me right now, we're going to have to suspend you, she said.

And although I tried to tell her that I'd forgot my glasses and that English wasn't my first language, I ended up being sent home anyway. On my way back, I couldn't help but wonder to myself: *Do large watery eyes naturally mean truth and honesty?* I didn't know then and I still don't know now. What I did know was that I was full of hate. I hated Ms. Carter for being blind and stupid, I hated myself for not having large watery eyes and better English, and finally, I hated how this stupid language had betrayed me. From that day onwards, I stopped talking.

CULTURAL DNA

Rich Rich Woman

Who do you want to be when you grow up is the last question on our second grade questionnaire. While the other kids are trying to wrap their brains around the question, I quickly jot down three words. I already know my answer by heart. I want to be a rich rich woman when I grow up.

I want to be a rich rich woman because they don't have to work or worry or only come home once a month. New clothes, Beyblades and Barbies they'll all be able to afford. They don't have to choose between work or family. Right? Rich rich women don't miss out on their daughter's childhood.

Hongyi and Hongyi

I never expected to meet another Hongyi in my entire life. I mean, it's a pretty niche name that doesn't really mean anything and there are like 14 million different combinations of characters or something, but I did. I don't know. I met Hongyi Lu just when I was starting to get used to introducing myself as Nicole. Just as I had started to give in to becoming the perfect Nicole. Just as I was beginning to let go of all the "Chinese" behind Hongyi.

I met Hongyi Lu in English. I remember how I ducked my head and cursed my parents when the teacher first called out the name "Hongyi." And amidst rolling my eyes and forcing out a reluctant "present," my thoughts were cut short as a tall Asian boy sprung from his seat, yelling, "IM HEREEEEE!" That was my first impression of him. Loud, proud and Chinese. Sometimes I still wonder to myself. How can he be so proud of simply being Hongyi?

Through our time spent in English class then, Hongyi Lu's enthusiasm and knowledge of our culture sent me into shame and reflection. Chinese culture was supposed to be both our cultures. Yet somehow, it felt like it was only his. I didn't know the myths he talked about nor the idioms he used and I felt stupid. I felt like an outsider looking in on something that was supposed to belong to me. Hongyi Lu stood out for his Asianness and he stood proud.

Perhaps because he was athletic and somewhat good-looking, Chinese culture suddenly became a hit in our school. Little infographic posters that used to be treated like scrap paper scattered across the ground were now restapled back on the bulletins and the pretty girls started showing up to festival events. Hongyi Lu made Chinese culture popular. He also made being Hongyi cool and it felt like a slap in the face. I know I shouldn't have cared that much because I'd never even introduced myself as "Hongyi" but I still felt like part of my identity had been robbed from me. Someone was using my name and doing it better. It really sent me thinking. Maybe I didn't have to be someone else to fit in. Maybe.

Schools

I first moved to New York when I was five. To Beijing when I was six. To Hong Kong by fourth grade. Back to Beijing by sixth grade. To Connecticut when I turned 13. And by age 14, I was in my seventh school. Sometimes I wonder what stability feels like.

I used to hate going to all these new schools because it meant that I had to give up everything I'd earned. All my friends, habits and relationships went down the drain and I had to somehow fill a new page up with memories. And those memories, inevitably, were going to go right back down the drain in three years. I hated moving. But I guess that sentiment changed when I grew older. It changed when I found that I could reshape myself to be anyone with any persona and be friends with any person because it wouldn't matter in the long term as I would be gone in a few years. And so it was. I became popular, emo, artsy, a bio-nerd, a gamer, a book-reading-loner. Space lets me turn to a new page and time makes people forget.

Sometimes I sit on the edge of the swing set in the corner of whatever new campus I'm on, sipping the same two flavors of Arizona tea I like and wondering what life would be like if I hadn't moved again. Wondering what it would feel like to be attached. Wondering what it would feel like if I wasn't constantly playing a game of trying to fit in.

Children

Children are the crystals borne out of the chemistry of love. Of course we love you, my mama would say whenever I asked her if she loved me.

I liked that saying. I liked it because it's funny, artistic and somewhat punny. Crystallization and chemistry, you know. But I guess more than that, I really entertained the idea of being the essence of their love. Something about that statement just made it sound like I was important and noticed. That I was more than just a byproduct of the love they had and didn't have to take care of, but a crystallization, the crux of their relationship.

But I wasn't a crystal borne out of the chemistry of their love. I was a test tube baby. A life forced to be alive. A planned little mistake that I thought had been an accident for the first 17 years of my life. I wish I was a crystal like everyone else.

CHAPTER II

Hong Kong

Spelling Test

Learned to learnt. Spelled to spelt. Fulfill to fulfil. All these words become red marks on my newest spelling test as I find myself placed in English B. Yet the spelling isn't wrong. At least not the way I was taught in New York nor the way I was taught back in Beijing. But here in Hong Kong, they are wrong.

You got placed in English B? One of the girls next to me scoffs.

We don't want this loser in our table, another one adds on.

There are literally like only like two English B classes with like 10 students in each, a random voice chimes in from somewhere.

I lower my head and try not to look at anyone. I've always prided myself on my ability to learn, my ability to remember, and most of all, my ability to spell. How can I go from winning the school spelling bee a year ago in to being placed in English B? Actually, I know the answer to that question. The difference is Hong Kong.

In Hong Kong, everything feels like a warped version of reality. Over here, the spelling is different for English. Here, the drivers drive on the right-hand side. Here, Chinese is also contorted into weird shapes and extra strokes as simplified characters become traditional. Everything is different in Hong Kong. And in that regard, Hong Kong has reshaped many of these small details in my life. Small details that often pass unnoticed until Grammarly underlines the way I spell "theatre" or "realise" in an essay. The mark Hong Kong has left on me lurks, and has scattered my subconscious mind the same way these British spellings in my writing do. I usually leave them be. I guess it's just kind of my way of remembering Hong Kong.

Martha and Hong Kong

Growing up, "treat others how you want to be treated" was my motto and bravery was my middle name. Or at least they were. They were until the Free Hong Kong campaign branded me permanent marks. Until the unification of hate under a single ideology drove all kindness and love out of the way. Until I met and unmet Martha.

2014 marked not only my arrival in Hong Kong but also the start of the war over supposed "freedom." Posters, smoke and shouting filled the skies and people filled the streets. Schools were shut down because of the campers in the middle of the roads. Central was a disarray of bodies and hatred plumed the air.

Get out of our streets, people yelled from their tents.

Get out of our land, people yelled on top of the mountains.

Get out of our country, people yelled, throwing eggs.

Get out. Get out. Get out.

And that was the way it was in Hong Kong. A constant struggle between the mainland authorities and the people fighting them and the poor, innocent others dragged in. Gun shots, spit, eggs and their eggshells, the floor was littered with pollution – the pollution of aggression and fear.

And that was the world I lived in. A mosh pit of hate, rage and violence – all together, creating a solid force of anger. The kind of anger that melts down family relationships; the kind of anger that solves nothing; the kind of anger that removes individuality. You were either one of them or you were the enemy. Worse yet, you were no one, not an individual. Not a person. Just the target of their rage.

Don't talk to anyone on your way to school, my mom said.

Don't look anyone in the eye, my mom said.

If they ask you if you're from Hong Kong, you nod and only speak in English, my mom said. Promise me you won't speak Mandarin outside of school, okay?

But I didn't speak Mandarin in school either. I didn't because all the boys would gang up on the kids from mainland the moment they spoke Mandarin.

Diu lei lo mo, they would spit.

It was Cantonese I didn't understand but had learned to look away from. I couldn't afford to be brave in Hong Kong. Not when any defense meant isolation and a drop of Mandarin could mean a beating. I learned to bite my tongue and look away.

The school was always big on some bullying prevention thing – they sent out a survey every other week and held an assembly every month. Nothing worked. Not when half the teachers turned a blind eye and looked away the same as I did. Not when no one wanted to get involved. Not when Martha's story got silenced.

I met Martha in my fifth year. She was kind, sweet and innocent. Her father worked in the Hong Kong administration as some sort of higher up – the kind where his name and face got plastered on a poster with a red cross on it. I don't remember his name. What I do remember is how Martha was treated in school. A black eye from falling off the swing *accidentally*. A bruise from walking into a wall *accidentally*.

Free Hong Kong, the kids chant.

Your family is the reason why we don't have freedom, they yell.

Another slap in the face, a kick in the gut, a pull of the hair. It's Martha getting beat up again in the middle of the school yard. And I don't believe that no teachers hear their chants or her yells. But I guess I can't judge because I'm acting like I'm deaf.

And that's the funny thing. People turn deaf when they act deaf for too long.

This is the eighth-ranked school in Hong Kong, we say when greeting visitors.

Look at how studious the students are! we advertise. Look at all the beauty, the brains, and the excellent academic preparation! It's the best of the best!

But beneath the shiny floors, beyond the flowers, and behind the books is a hell only mainland students see.

Help! You're oversensitive.

Help! You're imagining things.

Help, Martha whispers.

It's a chilly October morning when I last see Martha.

Please help me, Martha whispers, staring in the general direction of the pillar I was hiding behind. Another *accident* is going on. I look down at her body – her bruises are growing worse as the protests grow more violent.

Please help me, Martha whispers again, her voice ghastly. Her eyes are already losing focus as she whispers one more time. I know she isn't looking at me but I still shiver. I turn to walk away. I know better than to help.

And that was the last time anyone ever saw Martha. Three weeks later, we received an invitation to her funeral. She had decided life wasn't worth living anymore. She was only 12 that year. And I guess that's when a spark of rage lit the bottom of my guts because that's when I became a hater. I was only 12 that year. One of the boys who had beat her ended in a psych ward. He could barely stand the thought of her death. He was only 12 that year.

We were all only 12 that year. But what's another 12-year-old's life in the great revolution for freedom, right?

Little Black Room

My only escape from Hong Kong are the weekend trips back to Shenzhen. They let me take a quick breath of freedom before I have to go back to my daily struggles. Yet one of these times, we weren't allowed to go back.

I'm lying in the backseat of the van, dreading the dawning of Monday, when the security guards at the border stop us.

Identification please. One of the policemen glares down at my mama.

Dutifully, we hand in our IDs and are immediately taken hostage. A tall guy leads me to a security room alone. The room is dark and I am sat behind a little white table while four other guys surround me. An officer sits down in the chair across from me.

Did you know your family was involved in a financial fraud situation? he says.

No, I shake my head.

He leans into me and stares at my eyes. Are you sure about that?

I shake my head again.

Your family is going to end up in jail if you don't answer me honestly, he threatens. I'll ask you one more time. Is your family involved in a financial fraud situation?

With that, I burst into tears. Fine, fine, I confess, I say, sobbing.

One of the guys around me hands him a pen and a piece of paper.

I promise I didn't mean to lose the 20 dollars at the science fair, I cry.

Another 45 minutes later, I am let out of the little black room. Another 20 minutes later, my mama is let out of hers.

Ma'am, please take your child and return to Shenzhen. You are no longer permitted to cross the border to Hong Kong, the officer who interrogated me says.

My mama mutters something about the Chinese government needing a scapegoat. We return home and for the next five months, I am school-less.

My dad never came out of his little black room. No one knew if he was still alive.

CHAPTER III

Middle School

Connecticut

By 13, I lived in Connecticut. Not wanting to end up in China's administrative detention system like my dad, Mama and I flew out of the country.

I'm not really sure how one should describe what it was like to live in Connecticut. Trees, trees, water, trees, trees, more trees. Something like that. There was not much going on in Connecticut. And while it might not have been all that entertaining, at least it was better than being in the hell called Hong Kong. Yay everyone gets free speech and freedom, right?

School was the exact same way. There wasn't much happening in school. I mean, after all, it was just white boy, white girl, white girl, white boy, one Black kid, white boy, white boy, white girl, one Asian kid. Something about the lack of diversity mirrored the lack of nuance here. Connecticut would be unseasoned chicken if it was a food.

And how did I choose to deal with unseasoned chicken? I just existed in whatever form or fashion I was in and lounged the day away reading Chinese webnovels and painting my nails black. Connecticut made me boring.

Except there was stuff going on in Connecticut. Just way more silent than it was in Hong Kong. Physical abuse and fits of outrage were traded in for isolation and whitewashing. It's the unspoken rules that are more dangerous.

First Love

His eyes are blue like the sky. I've never seen eyes so blue.

Big, small, slanted, drooped, shining, brown, hazel, black, green, I've never seen eyes so blue. I tell him that his eyes are beautiful and he stares at me weird. I've never seen eyes so blue.

Leo never really talks to me in school because he's popular. Something about sports apparently makes you popular, when in China, it made you a failure. But Leo is popular and Leo is always talking and Leo sometimes stares at me.

I wonder why he stares at me but never figure out why. But before I realize, I'm wearing tennis skirts, Nike white socks, and I tie my hair in a ponytail the way he likes girls to wear their hair. Leo likes when I tie my hair in a ponytail. Every time Leo stares at me, I breathe a little harder and accidentally let a smile slip through my lips.

And then there's Olivia. Everyone says that Leo belongs with Olivia. I find out a week before the school dance that Leo likes Olivia. I find out a day before the school dance that Olivia said yes. I find out the day of the school dance that they kissed. I find out two days after the school dance that Leo has liked Olivia since the day that he met her. I guess that makes sense. I mean, Olivia is white, blonde, athletic and has eyes as blue as Leo's.

I wonder if Leo will like me if my hair is blonde and my eyes are blue. I really want blue eyes.

MADE

Four popular girls; an acronym of their initials; "MADE" was basically a remake of mean girls. See, when I first found myself in Connecticut, I never thought life would devolve into one of those stupid coming-of-age movies. Except it did. By some odd coincidence, these four shining, brilliant beauties were constantly vying to the death over some random boy's attention. Our own version of a burn book was written. Hair was pulled. Sides were picked. And eventually, there was a huge fallout and "E" got suspended. Good thing I was a little nobody in their fights. Bad thing the grade had to deal with the aftermath collectively. Popularity is kind of a joke. Except it's not. Silently, everyone subjugates themselves to it in one way or another. Fit in, fit in, fit in.

Bangs

Ozzy is beyond quiet when he sits in the corner of the classroom. That alone is enough to make him my friend. I'm shy in my language and stubborn in my unwillingness to talk, so anyone with the same understanding of silence feels like a breath of fresh air in the competitive world of who's louder. In that odd way, Ozzy and I appreciate each other.

And while Ozzy is odd in many ways, the one thing people usually ask Ozzy is about his long ginger curls and how they curtain his entire face.

How do you see through *that*? *Can* you see? Show us your eyes!

Stupid of them, really. I find it funny they expect Ozzy to reply. And I would be right because Ozzy doesn't reply. On the few occasions he does say something, he tells them it's because he wants to be blind. It never fails to make me smile.

For that reason, however, Ozzy remains faceless to me. He never offers to show and I never ask. Yet part of me is curious. Curious not because I want to know what he looks like but because I wonder if he keeps his hair long the same reason I keep my mouth shut – because I have somehow convinced myself that in my refusal to be part of the social cycle of judging and expressing, I can somehow escape and detach myself from society's critical eye.

I'm not sure if that's how Ozzy thinks. That's just how I think. But in our mutual respect for each other, Ozzy and I are friends.

Blue Eyes

I sit next to Leo in Latin class now because our eighth-grade Latin teacher seems to be convinced that he'll fail the class without me. I can't say I'm complaining because even though I'm pretty sure I'm over him, I still like to stare into his blue eyes. I like to draw his blue eyes. I would still like to be someone with blue eyes.

Leo tells me random things about his life. He says his friends aren't actually that nice. He says he's tired of sports. He says he doesn't actually like Olivia. I shake my head because I don't believe him for a second.

Why do you go to school dances with her, then? I ask.

Because our friends think we look good together, he says.

I shake my head again because I agree with his friends. Their blue eyes look really good next to each other. The clarity in their eyes intertwines to become a symbol of honesty and love. I think they must belong together.

Best Friends

Arielle is a song of music. Her every stride, step and glide follow an invisible rhythm that guides her through the day. I've never met someone so in tune with themselves. And the funny thing is, she used to be the "A" in "MADE." I guess she's not all that bad, not the way rumors made her out to be. With that, we became friends.

Come on Nicole, let's go to the practice rooms! I have a new idea for a song, she'd say, batting her pretty eyelashes.

Okay, okay, Arielle, run slower, Jesus. I'll be there, I'd shout back, my hand in hers as we make our way down to the school's music rooms.

There, we found heaven. Eighty-eight keys, an enclosed space and her angelic voice – we spent every afternoon composing. C chord, B chord, F chord, A chord, repeat. C chord, B chord, F chord, A chord, repeat. Simple progressions turned seventh-grade masterpieces and we bathed in delight as music bounced off our fingertips and lips.

I wish time could stay frozen, I'd say.

I wish we could always be best friends, she'd say.

Rainbow Pride

My mama tells me gay people are weird. She says that they live like animals. She says that being gay is a disease and that's why gay people can't control themselves. My mama tells me to not get close to the gay kids in my school. I'm not even sure if there are any gay kids in my school.

I turn out to be wrong because Devin is gay. Except that I completely missed the memo until he kissed a boy at summer camp. I mean, I'm not sure how I didn't know for so long but apparently, everyone else has known *forever.*

I find out later that it's because of the cloak on his back: Devin always wears a rainbow cloak like it's his superhero cape. *I've* always thought it's because he's an *artist* but apparently, it's because he's *gay.* Every single school day, Devin bounces down the hallway waving his cape around like a flag and every time I catch a glimpse of color rushing through the crowd, I know it means he's late for class. *Apparently,* it also means that he's gay. China didn't prepare me for the fact that rainbow means gay.

Devin and I are best friends. But for a moment, I'm not sure we are allowed to be friends anymore. I mean, although my mama won't admit it, I know she doesn't like him. Her pretty doe eyes lose their warmth when he comes around. I mean I knew she couldn't always have had a headache when he was here but I always just thought it was because he was a boy and mama doesn't like me around boys. Now I'm pretty sure it's because she always knew he was gay.

Video Games

Video gaming is my key to the online world. Mama doesn't like it when I spend a lot of time on the online world.

There are dangerous people on there, she says.

You never know what someone wants from you, she cautions.

Don't ever give them your real name, okay?

And I don't. I never give anyone my real name, nor my real picture, nor even my real favorite color. I delve deep into the addiction of being different people.

Nice to meet you, I'm Vivian! I'm Stephanie! I'm Violet! I'm Tiffany! I would say.

I feel safe in my anonymity and the online world soon becomes the safe haven of my self-exploration. I can be anyone I want to be. No one knows my name, my social status or what I look like. In fact, no one knows anything except what I am willing to tell them. And the best thing? When something doesn't work out and my facade falls apart, it only takes a matter of seconds to restart, reshape and redefine myself with a completely new group of people. Video gaming is my safe haven.

Brown Eyes

Somehow through Latin class, Leo and I have started to become friends. I think I know more about him than any of his friends. His favorite color is blue. His favorite candy is Jolly Ranchers. His favorite number is seven because he was born in July. And for some odd reason or another, Leo likes to lean his head on my shoulder during class while he talks to me.

You're kinda pretty, Leo says. I laugh at him because I don't believe him.

I really like your eyes, Leo says. I laugh at him because I don't believe him.

I think I might like you, Leo says. I laugh at him because I don't believe him.

And even though I say I don't believe him, I know a part of me wonders whether Leo actually likes me. I wonder if he wants to hold my hand. I wonder whether he and I might go to the dance together. I wonder what his lips taste like.

With my lenience comes a Leo who starts to push my boundaries. His head is now always on my shoulders. His knees nudge mine. Sometimes he holds my hand underneath the table.

Nicole, I like you, Leo says. I don't laugh anymore because I want to believe him.

His hands start to crawl up my thighs and sometimes his other hand goes around my waist. Sometimes they start to find their way up my shirt and skirt. I try to push him off. It never works.

I wish you were white so I could date you, Leo says. I don't laugh because I know my eyes will never be blue like Olivia's.

It's spring already when a girl named Riley finally sees Leo's hands try to go places I don't want them to be. Riley screams. Riley screams and the whole class holds their breath as she screams. And before her scream ends, the whole school knows. They know me as the girl who is desperately trying to break up Leo and Olivia. Leo and I don't talk anymore. They know me as the girl Olivia cries about. Leo tells me that I'm crazy for believing that he actually liked me. The whole school knows me as the Asian whore. Leo tells me that he never wants to talk to me again.

Necklaces

My least favorite gift to receive is a necklace. And it's not because I hate jewelry or whatever, it's just that when someone gives you a necklace, it means that they didn't care enough to find out about who you actually are and what you actually like. And no, giving other types of jewelry is different. To give an anklet or bracelet or ring, you'd at least have to know the measurements. But a necklace? Not only is it usually a one-size-fits-all, but people like my mama also have a collection of 30 random necklaces sitting at home ready to be given out for occasions and birthdays.

Every single year, for every single birthday, I receive multiple necklaces. One from my uncle, one from my aunt, one from my dad's coworker 1, one from my dad's coworker 2, and one more from my dad. And every single year I look down at these beautiful chains, each ingrained with a beautiful gem of some sort, and sigh. It's just not what I want. I hate to sound ungrateful, but I would rather have any of them spend a quarter of the money to get me a pair of shoes, a year of Spotify premium, or even a gift card for some video game I play. But none of them seem to know anything about me. Not that I'm a sneakerhead, not that I'm a gamer, not that I could be anybody other than a girl who they subconsciously associated with the word "necklace." I hate receiving necklaces.

I hate receiving necklaces so much that I've started to try and experiment. I began to throw hints about disliking them, choosing to give other types of gifts for people's birthdays, and even straight up telling my dad that I didn't want him to give me a necklace for my birthday.

Inevitably, I received another necklace on my birthday. It's like I'm talking to air. And sometimes I wonder if he heard what I said and has just brushed it off, thinking he'll remember it but end up forgetting to mention it to his secretary who, realistically, is the person getting me the gifts. I don't hate necklaces. I just wish people would listen to what I have to say.

Changes

For the first time in my life, I finally know what Ozzy looks like because today Ozzy has tied his ginger hair into a ponytail and cut his bangs. I stare in curiosity. His freckles sprinkle across his face like pixie dust and his eyes are green like the willow trees that grow around the edges of the koi ponds. His green eyes are soft like spring. I'm staring when he writes down five letters. N-E-O-M-A.

It's pronounced nn-ai-OH-m-uh, he says.

N-ai-OH-m-uh, I echo silently in my head.

Neoma, he says again. That's my new name.

Neoma, I whisper after him.

Neoma, he smiles, Neoma like the new moon.

Neoma, I think to myself. Neoma who's a pretty girl. Neoma who likes pink. Neoma who blossoms crayon dust into fishes and birds and whales in my notebook. Neoma who stuck with me even though the whole school hated me because of Olivia. There isn't Ozzy anymore. Just Neoma with long ginger curls and green eyes like willow leaves.

Treasure Trove

I keep a treasure trove of letters in a battered Adidas shoebox under the third nook of my bookshelf. Inside, tucked away, is a safe haven for feelings, fears and anxieties. Every scribble is a silent thought that I'm too afraid to think out loud. Every "I love you" is one that I'm too afraid to say out loud. Every apology is one that I'm too proud to lower my head for and put it out to the world. My writing is my home.

I like writing letters because it almost feels like they'll actually go somewhere. That someone like Kitty in *To All the Boys I Loved Before* will see the names and addresses and stamps I put on and send my feelings out to the world. That somehow by writing all these letters I'll be able to get the closure I deserve by myself. I love writing letters.

For once in my life, I can be honest about how I feel. Screw the different personas, screw the different people I temporarily become while I try to fit in. Screw the fear of admitting weaknesses. I can just be honest. Honesty runs pretty thin nowadays. Especially when it's so easy to get carried away in a lie that makes me happy. Afterall, what's better than simply believing you're always right and always satisfied?

I reread all my letters every time a new one is added in. I breathe in the scenarios and feelings they paint and wonder how I could feel so differently about something and someone once upon a time. How did I love them so much? How did I hate them so much? Why was I even worried? I don't know, but it's refreshing to see how sometimes my words remember tougher times differently to how my memories do.

Pride Parade

Come with us, it'll be fun, Devin says.

No, I have an essay, I say.

Come with us, it's summer, Devin says

No, I have an essay, I say.

Devin wraps his rainbow cloak around me and I let him hold my hand and drag me up.

Devin calls this little bunch of people downtown the pride parade. They walk around with a speaker and flaunt their hair and huge posters. The sound of *Born This Way* echoes through the entire street and their shoes squeak a symphony of pride. Devin fits right into the group when we get there but I stay back because people on the side of the street are looking at us weird.

For a second, I see my mother's eyes in an Asian woman staring at us weirdly. Every single breath inside me dies and I huff out a thread of dread. All I want is for her to stop looking at me. I want to leave. I want to explain. I stutter, grasping for words but she turns away. Words foam in my mouth.

I don't know why I'm upset. Maybe because I feel like my mother is disappointed in me or maybe because I don't want to be grouped as gay. Maybe it's because I don't want to be a gay little girl with short spikey hair, a nose ring and a graphic T screaming *Born This Way*.

I tell myself I don't belong here. I'm not one of these people. I'm not gay. I want to be normal. I clutch Devin's little pride flag closer to me. I'm never going to pride again.

Chopsticks

In China, they say that if you hold your chopsticks closer to the thinner end, you're closer to your dad's side of the family. That must not be true because even though I've tried so hard to hold my chopsticks that way, I don't even remember what my dad looked like when I was younger. And nowadays, memories of him are frozen in fragments of time. Fragments of 1 am visits back home, of occasional dinners, and of when he would bellow in laughter when I won an award. And in those fragments, he would kiss my forehead and I would let myself get lost in the moment, believing that he loved me. But in truth, my dad knows almost nothing about me just as how I've grown, eventually, to know nothing about him.

I used to know everything about my dad. I knew small things like his favorite color and core elements like his life philosophies. I knew his childhood and I knew his work struggles. I even spent hours researching his horoscope. I really wanted to know my dad. And I guess some part of him wanted to know me as well because of the once or twice he did get to see me, every couple of months, he would ask me what my favorite food was, what my favorite book was, and what my favorite color was. But I guess for the everchanging nature of a child, his interest in me was never quite frequent enough to "know" me.

I don't hold my chopsticks closer to the thinner end anymore. My mama never liked it because I used to get food all over my hands – I was never a neat eater. And since it's harder like that way anyway, I just gave up on him and gave into what's easier.

The Scammer

I met Chapelle on the streets of New Haven when he stormed down Whalley Avenue blasting rap music on his speakers, handing out papers for his commissions. And I guess I must've looked like some sort of preppy, rich, inexperienced doll, perfect for his business because he came straight for me without hesitation.

Hi, ma name's Chapelle, he said. I work commissions around the corner so the children that live on the other side of that hill can read. We gotta get outta this place, my friend, we gotta get them books and that education. I be reading these children books and I just know you wanna help. Cuz ya know what they be lookin' like? They ma people. They ma lil boysboys, lil Hispanic boys and children with skin like yours. They're your people. I ain't here for no campaign, no bullshit, no donations or whateva, I'm just here to support the community. We gotta get our people educated. My lil sister – I got her name tattooed right here, her name's Mari – she's your age and beggin' for school. What's you name, pretty? Oh it's Kat? Well nice to meet you Kat, ma name's Chapelle. I finna change the world with what I can, Kat, and I just need your help.

Chapelle handed me the piece of paper for his commissions. 50 dollars, 100 dollars, 150 dollars, 325 dollars, 500 dollars, the commission money skyrocketed with every line I read.

You wanna help the children who can't afford an education, don't you? You know spending money for their books is worth it. Kat, I can tell you'll be able to help.

But I wasn't. I wasn't able to help because I'm not the trust-fund baby Chapelle was looking for. I was just a young girl trying her best to fit into her predominantly white school. I wasn't able to help because living in China for 13 years has taught me how to identify a scam. I wasn't able to help because my name isn't Kat, his shirt said he was a scammer in Chinese and I don't actually work down the road. But I wanted to help. I wanted to help because his use of rhetoric was better than everyone in my Athenian Democracy class. I wanted to help because I knew he wasn't lying about having a little sister named Mari or how the children were struggling. The light in his eyes told me he would put the money to them if he didn't have family to feed first. I would have got scammed by him if I had the money on me.

I left Chapelle with the truth. He screamed after me that I was a racist bigot. I screamed back thank you. In a weird way, Chapelle made me want to change the world to be a better place. I respected him. For the brief moment that our lives intersected, I got a glimpse of the inequalities in just the small city we both live in. Someone should've paid for his college education because he would've made it far. I can't. But as far as I know, I can read for children the way he wishes he had the time to. I can dedicate the money from my books to their education. I think Chapelle is part of the reason I want to change the world.

Drawing

Watching colors bloom in my sketch book is a new pastime. I think it all started because I wanted to capture a moment of beauty before it was gone. Beauty is often very fleeting. A person only lives one lifetime. A flower only blooms one season. You can never relive a moment twice. I'd like to put it on paper.

I guess I prefer drawing more than photos because photos are too rigid. Photos, unlike memories, beauty and drawings, stand as the stone-hard truth and I much prefer the hope and possibility of fluidity. I guess that is to say it's not about the moment that happens in front of you. It's about finding my version of the moment in me. In my pens. In my colors. In my sketchbook. In me.

On my wall is a stretch of sketches. Arielle, Leo, Martha, Mama, my dad, me. Everyone captured in a moment as I like to remember them. Arielle when we're writing songs. Leo before he left me. Martha when she smiled. My mama when she cooks. My dad. Not really. I don't have an image of him I'd like to freeze in time.

What If

What would you do if your parents got a divorce? Aunty Margaret asks.

What do you mean what would I do if my parents got a divorce? I ask back.

I don't know, just like, what would you do? she says.

I've never considered it, I say, and I won't until that day comes.

You've just never considered the possibility of that happening? she pushes again.

Hey, do you have something you want to tell me? I ask. Never mind that. I know there's something Margaret wants to say to me. Are my parents okay? I ask again before she replies.

No, no, no, they're totally fine! I was just wondering, she says.

I guess I would probably cry really really really hard and then never talk to my dad again, I say.

Aunty Margaret doesn't bring the topic up ever again.

A Photo's Evidence

Air runs thin as I zoom into the photo, eyes locked onto the tiny reflection in the back of the mirror. I cannot believe it. Everything is in front of me.

My dad sent us this photo while allegedly on a business trip. Everything about this photo seems so subtly wrong. The lack of wrinkles – his skin has been blurred. The oddly pale color of his hands – a filter has been applied. And finally, the mirror that revealed another chair in front of him – he was with another woman. And from the saturation of the filter, I immediately know that she is at most in her late twenties. Maybe early thirties.

So that's what people have been hinting at. I let my brain wander. What if I have misunderstood? What if I am just being oversensitive? Yet no matter how hard I try to believe otherwise, I know I am right. All the occasional glances I've got from family friends, weird facial expressions when I mentioned my dad, and rumors that once danced in the mouths of relatives have all been real.

I sit still and let suffocation clench my throat. My chest tightens as I try to click away, to tear my eyes from the photo and forget about it. But I can't. What happens to my family now? What happens to home? What happens to me?

You have to fix it, a voice inside of me urges, you're the only one who can keep this relationship together. You're the only tie they have of their love.

You have to tell your mother about it, my other voice says. She deserves to know. You know this is all your fault. Their relationship would've never fallen apart had your mother not come to the United States for you. The least you can do is tell her.

I wish I never knew.

Katarina

I've been calling myself Katarina since seventh grade. Well, I mean I found the name back then but it wasn't until high school before I actually started going by it. And the funny thing is, it actually all started as a joke. A joke about some prank that I needed another name for and, after a whole weekend of playing *League of Legends*, the first name I blurted out was Katarina. And I guess from then was when I truly noticed how much I connected with the name: a lone assassin fighting for her homeland, Katarina is red-headed, bold, unapologetic, calculating and decisive – everything I wanted to be. Almost as a hope to inherit some of her charisma then, Katarina became my first pen name. To my joy, my writing under that name grew stronger, sharper and more effective. Anyone reading my works back then would see how my language took a liking upon her daggers and became a weapon to destroy everything in sight.

Over time, Katarina started to change. I became more Katarina and Katarina became more me. Still bold and decisive, we were less sharp and more deliberative. I was starting to become the leader that the name Katarina called for. And I was really happy being just that. As I grew more confident and assertive, the image other people had of me also grew to be stronger. I was finally who I wanted to be and no longer unsure of myself. I know who I am.

Nice to meet you, I'm Katarina.

Writing

Sometimes I sit down to write, my hands on my keyboard, ready to sing the tunes of my heart with each drumming tap. Yet my eyes wander away. They stare without purpose, through the farthest branch of my window, through the blazing sun, to the washed-out blue of the sky. My eyes take my soul away to drift. They race in their freedoms and run off like teenage couples as they make friends with the wind, and dart through the negative space formed by the silhouette of thin branches.

How does one write? People say words flow like music to your fingertips; it's a magical hush, gracing through the pages. But mine never danced. They stood rigid. Like a painting without highlights, a song without grace notes, an actor without passion. My words stand tall, never bowing down, always too sharp, and too dangerous for my own liking.

Sometimes I look down to my hands as I write, as I force one more word through the rage of my veins. I flush these feelings out of my system with each pump of my blood, heartbeat and breath. My hands turn purple with bruises. These words cut into my delicate flesh. They are daggers ready to stab, and with each strike, a mirage falls apart, leaving nothing behind but a myriad of broken dreams trying to fill that indescribable void.

Sometimes, on a day like today, I sit alone, trying to put the heat of my blood onto a page, but I can't. So I sit, my mind sprawled over its conflicting reign, trying to process the creation and destruction of each world I conjure up in a matter of seconds. Why do I write? I stand, staring off to nowhere, letting the rain meet my skin, slowly drowning me in silence as my mind fills to the brim.

Water drips into my overfilled capsule with endless enthusiasm, and hot streaks roll off my cheeks. Everything drains out as my eyes trace the lines of another mastered symphony blasting Wham! into my world. I lose myself as each syllable rolls off my tongue, etching a new tattoo within me. I want to sing lullabies with my words and set sky lanterns free. And so I write.

I know my words can be fierce. They rush into a battlefield like soldiers too tired of waiting for an order to begin their bloodshed. I know they don't care to wear the armor of subtleties, or correct their indelicacies when they can pierce through the mind. I hated writing. I hated my own words. Yet I still sit down, beating my mind up as I try to scribble words across a blank page. I write for the sake of staring into my soul. I write to put my burning rage and hatred for the world down on a piece of paper and to scorch myself awake. I write to criticize. After all, how can we choose not to write – when words are all we have?

The Scarier Side of the Neighbourhood

I wouldn't call my mama racist because she isn't. I mean, she isn't racist in the sense that she would never curse someone out for being a different skin color. She isn't racist in the sense that she believes everyone should get an even chance at life. Yet still, deep rooted somewhere, something always makes her walk faster in what she calls the "scarier side of the neighbourhood."

Don't look around, Nicole, she says.

Keep your eyes to your feet and walk faster, she says.

You never know if you're going to get shot in a place like this, she says.

But Mama, I complain, there's not even anyone out on the street I say. Yeah, it might be an all-Black neighbourhood but that doesn't mean it's any more dangerous.

You give me a single crime rate statistic that suggests otherwise, she scolds.

I look down at my shoes and keep walking.

CHAPTER IV

High School

Camila's World

It's almost an unspoken rule nowadays that every grade needs a girl like Olivia. And since our Olivia left for California because her daddy retired, the new girl Camila has taken her spot.

The boys at school think Camila's too beautiful to be real because of her soft blonde hair, ocean blue eyes, and laugh that sounds like a thousand ringing bells. The girls at school think Camila is too fake to be true because of her soft blonde hair, ocean blue eyes, and laugh that sounds like a thousand ringing bells. I think Camila is nicer than Olivia. Partially because Camila told me my blue hair was "savage" and partially because Camila doesn't care to entertain boys like Leo.

The thing is, Camila doesn't realize she is the Olivia of our grade. And while the boys flutter around her like bees around a flower, Camila simply reads her books and hums her songs. Her inattentiveness to their pleas for a mate somehow makes her that much more attractive. Everything she does becomes glorified: when Camila doesn't like sports, it's probably because she's girly and posh. When Camila doesn't do make up, it's probably because she's chill and casual. I don't know. When I don't like sports or don't do my makeup, I'm usually just a nerd who's too lazy to look good.

But no matter what they like to think, the boys at school know nothing about Camila. They don't know that she tries her hardest to avoid parties and alcohol. Nor that she hates mingling with crowds. And definitely not the fact that she's anorexic and that's why she hesitates every time she picks up lunch. They just love the version of Camila they have projected in their heads. The boys at school are way too caught up in her blue eyes.

Yet somehow, in some way, Camila is also way too caught up with herself. Not in the way that's hugely narcissistic, but in the subtle way that she believes that she has it worse than anyone else. Camila talks to me about her problems. Every other week, I have her sobbing into the phone, talking about the trauma her middle school bullies imprinted on her. I wish I knew how to comfort her but I don't. Instead, I stay silent because I don't know how to tell her. I don't know how to tell her that life gets much worse than some white boy who has a crush on her telling her that she's ugly because he's 12. I don't know how to tell her that I've seen people beaten to a pulp for speaking Mandarin and not Cantonese. I don't know how to tell her that my middle school classmate took 50 pills and disappeared after the last time she reached out to me but I was too afraid to step in. I don't know how to tell her anything. And so I just smile. Smile and bring Camila some hot water and give her a hug because she'll probably never have to see this side of the world anyway.

Somebody to Someone

I could've been somebody, you know? My mama sighs. And I know. I know because my mother is the most brilliant woman I know. She is smarter than my dad, smarter than her entire class, and smarter than all her siblings. I know because my mama and my father made it out of the rural towns with only cents in their pockets. I know because my mother is like her name –proud like the lofty mountains.

Sometimes I wish my mama had never taken up the role of taking care of me because I don't want to hear how she could've been somebody to someone. I shut my eyes close and clench my jaw way too tight when I hear the yearning in her voice.

I just wish I hadn't given up on my life so early, she says.

I wish I still worked, she says.

Your father would still respect me if I hadn't quit my job, she says.

And I understand. I understand because I know my mama is a proud woman. I know because she changed the last character of her name when she quit. Changed it from the pride of the mountains to the gentleness of feathers. Changed it when she thought people no longer needed a strong woman out of her. Changed it when she chose home instead of herself.

And I just hug my mama and don't say anything. I don't say anything because I know words won't change her mind. I don't know how to tell her that she is somebody to someone. She is my world. She's my Uncle Feng's support system. She's the star that everybody in her family looks up to. She is somebody to so many people but she's blind sighted, trying too hard to be somebody to my dad. I know nothing I say will change her mind, so I swallow my words and just hug her. Every once in a while, staring up through my skylight at 2 am blasting Wham! on my computer, I wish being somebody to me would be enough for my mama.

Music Composition

Arielle and I stopped talking when freshman year started. I guess I hadn't realized it at the time, but everyone was automatically signed up for the new popularity contest when we joined freshman year. Arielle excelled at it. All her efforts trying so hard to put "MADE" away dissipated the moment new blood rushed the grade. Mondays she gossiped with Sarah, Tuesdays she flirted with Jackson, Wednesdays she watched the soccer games, Thursdays she hung out with Camila, and Friday she played piano with me. Except the Fridays got shorter and shorter and weekly composition days turned monthly, and monthly turned never. Arielle and I stopped talking three months into the school year. She had removed me the same way she removed music from her life.

I can't say I didn't hate her for it. Now practice room Fridays were spent alone – me and our 88 keys. Me and our songs. Me and our memories that only one of us wanted to cherish. Was I not enough? I don't know. But what I do know is that although Arielle disappeared from our music room, her lessons stayed with me. *A full cadence will sound more complete. Legato means slow and continuous. Motifs will give music structure.* My music moved from the Notes app on our phone to MuseScore to Guitar band and finally to Logic. I wrote my own song, Arielle. Are you proud of me?

Football Manager

Cold liquid traced the edges of my face as I glared upwards into Gary's sneering face.

"Get me another, freshman," he taunted.

No one wanted to be the football team's manager. First it was just an assembly announcement, then it was a schoolwide email, and finally, it was individual talks to every kid who didn't have a sport. Still, no one signed up. It's easy to explain why – either you had a sport, or you were a theatre and arts kid, and everybody knew the divide between the arts kids and the football kids. Never mind that the school had said they were going to build a stage for 15 years and instead refurbished the football field, just look on paper: artistic, intellectual and liberal versus athletic, well-off and conservative. None of it worked

You just can't be both, one of my friends said. They're just too different.

As a rising freshman just entering high school, the easiest route was to choose one. But I didn't want to choose. Implicit limitations and supposed divides of social construct were ridiculous and I refused to be confined by them. Plus, it was different this year – another freshman girl had forced her way onto the team as the first female football player in our school. I looked up to her, and so, following her lead, I signed myself up to be the football team's manager.

I regretted my decision within the first 30 seconds of practice. I was a singular ninth grade girl standing amidst forty 200-pound "boys." Unfortunately, I didn't speak football: basic terms such as "dab me up" and "caught a dub" alone took me a few weeks to get. Moreover, I was assigned none of the things a typical sports manager did – they didn't let me keep the score, run the balls, record practices or even sort out the Gatorade during the games. It was like I didn't exist.

"Maybe I shouldn't have signed up," I sighed to Andrea, the only other girl, on the bus ride to the second away game.

"Don't worry," she told me, "they'll get to know you. But first of all, you have to show them that you're willing to be one of them. Trust me, if you endure the hazing, they'll respect you."

On our game that day, Gary, the star player, called for Gatorade during a 15-second break. Amidst the mess of another player getting injured, no one heard him. I seized the opportunity and ran him the Gatorade. I wasn't supposed to do that.

"Here," I said, handing the purple liquid to him.

"That's not your job," he jeered. "Go sit back down and do nothing."

I ignored him and handed him the Gatorade again. Gary laughed and poured the Gatorade over my head. I was fuming.

"Go grab me another," he said.

I shut my mouth and did just that. Except this time around, when he reached his hand out for the Gatorade, I told him, "I don't run Gatorade for star players who can't even shoot the gap," before leaving.

Gary hollered in laughter and patted me on the back. "You've really got some nerve, freshman."

Since then, my place in the football team changed. Maybe it's because I was picking up their language or maybe everyone suddenly had a change of heart, but I slowly became part of the team. Players began to acknowledge my presence and took turns explaining how the game was played. Ironically, I was also assigned Gatorade duty. And in truth, while I might not be a talented football interpreter, I did make a good manager – I concocted the perfect mix of electrolytes and water and could fill up 40 cups of it more efficiently than any "water boy" they'd had before.

The Whole Story

Conversations on and off the football field slowly drew Andrea and I together. She taught me new football plays and I taught her color theory – we grew inseparable. It was another three-hour-long away trip to a football game when we randomly started talking about the whole Leo thing. I mean, I guess she'd probably heard about it already from the sidelines way back when, but she was the first person to know the whole story.

Andrea never understood why I had kept it down. I guess given her personality, she probably would've already done something about it. But I was different. Different because years of living in Hong Kong taught me how to shut up, years of trying to tell my story forced me to know better. Arielle made me know better. Camila made me know better.

Why didn't you tell someone about Leo earlier? Andrea asks.

I didn't because I knew no one was going to take it seriously, I say.

What do you mean no one would take it seriously? she asks again, it's clearly a big deal. Like if you had told me a year ago, *I* would've taken it seriously.

I laugh. Andrea frowns and shakes her head.

I laugh again. Well you know Arielle, right, like my ex-best friend? I ask.

Andrea nods. Right, the singing girl, she says.

Yeah, her, I say. Well, I remember mentioning it briefly to her way back when. And you know, she just told me that I was lucky to have a guy as attractive as Leo lay his hands on me.

That's not okay, Andrea says.

I just shake my head. I hadn't even told Andrea about Camila's reaction yet.

Camila had figured it was just some middle school thigh-touching and a little more. I mean I guess that was what it was. Camila had told me I was freaking out about nothing. I guess I was overreacting. I don't know. I haven't even kissed someone yet.

English Teacher

Your writing lacks purpose. Like, it's good in every other way – your descriptions are neat, ideas are cool, sentence structures are largely coherent – but your writing isn't motivated. Sit down for a moment. Why would I rather read your piece than anyone else's? Nicole, give me a reason to keep reading.

I take a deep breath in, trying to not blow up as I read through Mr. Luceria's comments for my essay. With every new word I take in, I grow a little more upset and by the end of his paragraph, I'm doing all I can to suppress the annoyance slowly blazing up my chest. *Your writing lacks purpose.* What is purpose in writing even supposed to look like? I mean, like, that's not even fixable. Sure, I can detail better descriptions, synthesize better ideas and work on better sentence structures. But how the hell can I make my writing have a purpose? I mean, what makes Shakespeare any more worth reading? And what about Montaigne? He's basically just a blogger in the Renaissance. What makes any of their writing any more or less special?

I write for the critical eye and I know. I can write analysis, I can write research papers, and I can write discussion questions. But when it comes to a story, I find myself lost, stumbling around in the letters of the page not knowing how to find myself. My writing inherited a hate, fury and lust for change in Hong Kong. With that stripped, who am I? For the first time, I feel stuck. I feel stuck because I don't know how to make my writing more purposeful. Stuck because maybe that is what my writing is like – lacking purpose – and I have no tools on hand to do anything about it.

'Mid' Asian Friend

Every hot white girl has a mid Asian friend. They are always inseparable. They go to parties together, watch football games together, visit boys' houses together. They're practically attached. Nobody likes the mid Asian friend but they know they all have to deal with her. One wrong move and you don't get the hot girl's Snapchat anymore.

I am the indispensable green leaf to Camila's flower. I follow her around everywhere and listen to all her problems, troubleshooting whatever might come her way. I don't remember the last time someone walked up to us and actually wanted to talk to me and not her. And that was the way we functioned.

Can I have your friend's number? they'll ask.

Do you think you guys will have time to hang out this Friday? they'll say.

Hey, can you possibly give me one period of space alone to make a move on Camila if I buy you some Arizona green tea? they'll bargain.

And that was the way we functioned. Green leaf and flower. She was my key to popularity and I was her key to beauty. I mean, beauty only exists under comparison, right?

Sam I Call Samantha

His name is Sam but I always call him Samantha. And I mean, Sam isn't feminine and Sam isn't soft. I just like to call him Samantha because I want to get a reaction out of him. I never do – but I call him Samantha anyway.

Sam and I talk about everything. Family, friends, relationships, favorite colors, favorite foods, least favorite people, lines from *The Lady of the House of Love*, why *Northanger Abbey* is fake gothic. Sam I talk about everything, and I look up to Sam because he's much older, but Sam and I aren't close. We aren't close because Sam doesn't have emotions. Sam is perfectly fine alone. I don't even know why I'm one of the few people he keeps around.

Sometimes I like to think of Sam as a singular carnation in the middle of the woods. I think about him like that because that's how he is: strong, proud and alone amidst bushes and bushes of roses and strawberries. *Dianthus caryophllyus*. Sam grows best in the full sun where he hides nothing from this world and carries the carnation's distinct, unapologetic scent. Sam names himself king in a kingdom where he lives alone.

I remember when Sam used to tell us stories about the people he's been with. Joanna, Natalie, Natasha, Carrie, Isabel, some random girl he doesn't remember the name of in Florida. And each time, I would gawk at his comfortably reckless disposition. I secretly want to be like Sam. I want to be like Sam because nothing seems to be able to hurt him. Not a single person and not a single comment.

It's also true that perhaps I find comfort in Sam's lack of emotions. Something about his emotionless self makes me feel safe. Safe in the sense that he won't ever judge me and that I would never disappoint him because he never cared about me in the first place and therefore expects nothing from me.

Life must be so much more bearable when you can't be disappointed or sad, right? I think that's why Sam always laughs. I think that's why we are such good friends. I think that's why I call him Samantha.

Yellow and a Splash of Neon Blue

Sam is always laughing. He laughs when I tell him a bad joke; he laughs when the sky is particularly blue; he laughs when his cat nudges him. Sam says he laughs because there's no reason not to, but I think he laughs because he finds crying is pathetic. Sam laughs when he loses a bet; he laughs when one of his friends leaves him; he laughs when someone asks for his money. And that's how it always is. Sam is always laughing. But a year ago sometime, something about Sam's laugh changed. For a brief moment, his laugh became real. Real and not just an exercise of 17 tired muscles. For just a moment, I could almost see a spark light up his eyes. And while I wish I could say this spark lasted, it was gone almost as fast as it came. His spark was named Charlotte.

I don't understand why Sam chose Charlotte. She wasn't pretty or particularly bright. She was struggling with a terrible father and couldn't seem to even mildly pull herself together. Charlotte was everything not up to my standards in finding Sam a girl. And no matter how much I pestered Sam about her, he simply closed his eyes and dived into it. I got one 5 am phone call when he was driving eight hours to see her and another 4 am one saying that she had dumped him. I couldn't let go. I wanted to know what made Charlotte so special, so deserving of a love as dedicated as Sam's, and so I kept asking. Finally, on some random night during spring break, Sam cracked.

I guess Charlotte just reminded me of when life used to have color, Sam says, before I stopped caring and things actually felt like it was going somewhere.

What happened? I ask.

Clove happened, he says.

Clove? I echo.

Yeah, he says, she's the girl I got engaged to when I was 18.

But she's not in your life anymore, I say.

No, he repeated, but I never stopped loving her anyway. She was the most brilliant person I've ever met. She was like if yellow was a person. And I guess that's why we worked in the first place – because she's yellow and I'm a splash of neon blue.

And why didn't it work out? I ask.

I don't know, he says. I guess one of our best friends had a stupid crush on her for years and he went insane when we got engaged. He and she and one of my other friends went up a hill one day and the three of them just never came back down.

She ran away with him? I ask.

No, Sam shook his head, I had to go to their funerals. And then one more when the only other friend in our group couldn't deal with it. And then I left the town and never came back either.

And Charlotte? I murmur.

She's like a hint of yellow I guess, he says.

And then it clicked for me. What color am I? I ask.

A spark of neon blue, he smiles.

Red

I don't think I'm a spark of neon blue at all. I say that because I don't feel like I'm brilliant or bright or dashing in the way neon blue suggests. Not at all. I tend to think of myself as red. I don't know if it's because I've been told my entire life that I resemble some sort of warm color and I've taken that to heart or because I actually think so. Regardless, I think I've grown quite fond of red. Red is the color of passion. Red is also the color of China, of stop signs, of traffic lights, of roses, of fear, of pain, of love, of pride, of hate, of rage and of control. Red is grounded and red is dangerous. I guess some part of me likes the idea that I'm in control of my own life and that's why I fell in love with red. But I don't think I was born red. Red never coursed through my veins the way it did my grandfather's, or my cousin's. Part of me thinks I was born a spark of neon blue, free and hopeful. I think that's what Sam sees in me. I also think that's what my Aunt Nenny fell in love with.

Talent

I hate when people say that I'm talented at arts not because I'm not. Or at least what they see behind each brush stroke, rhyme and joke I create isn't talent. It's hours and hours of passion, rage, sweat, tears and hope. Yet somehow, all these individual struggles of emotions become all swept up under the tongue and turn into talent. I guess it's just because talent sounds more like a difference in luck and genetics than a difference in persistence. Or maybe because talent is easier to blame.

You're just so talented, they say.

You never seem to have to try, they say.

I wish I was as talented as you, they say.

Yet when I write, I'm squeezing words out like they're dirt particles in a half-dry rag. Yet when I draw, I'm standing in an empty world trying to sketch with my eyes blinded. Yet when I perform, I'm six feet deep in Antigone's grave trying to understand why she cares so much about the burial of her brother. Nothing of art comes easy. I hate being called talented. Maybe because I'm simply not. Or maybe because talent means nothing without the hours.

Yet when I eventually plateau in the depth of some art block, crying away hours because my brushes can't seem to bring to life the same eyes they once did, people have the audacity to call me a genius that didn't live up to my potential.

Why didn't you just try harder, they say.

You were so talented, they say.

I hate when people say that I'm talented.

Uncle John

Uncle John puffs out another sigh of smoke. I watch as the thin strands of silver mist slither out of his nose and mouth and coil around his hands, hissing silently. These wisps slowly twirl upwards as the sorrow and memories they hold simmer and disperse with it, leaving behind only the sickly-sweet scent of strawberries. He tells me not to tell other people that he smokes but I don't know why he even asks because I don't care.

Uncle John used to be a musician of some sort before life got him good. Uncle John tells me to not pursue art because art makes nobody any money and art can't pay bills. I simply nod. I nod because it doesn't matter to me. I nod because I know I will never be able to give up art the way he did. I nod because I'm my only family.

Sometimes I wonder who Uncle John could've been if he hadn't let life take a hold of him. I imagine he would be in the front row of the orchestra with his violin in hand, smiling as notes dance off his bow. I imagine he would bask in applause. I know he would be proud because you can see the pride in his eyes every time he lets memories of his past slip loose. I imagine these things from the way dust sits on his old music theory books, from the way he chugs his whiskey, and from the way he named his daughter Melody. Melody, the center thread of every musical piece. Melody, the soothing tunes that are meant to inspire hope, ease anxieties and arouse passion. I wonder if that's what his daughter means to him.

I imagine a lot because I don't want to be like him, a wasted artist at age 45 wishing he had chosen himself. Yeah. That's how I think of him. I think of him as an old artist. An old, lost artist trapped in the body of a middle-aged old man, who sits by his barbecue grill cooking away his nostalgia and puffing away memories.

Uncle John's smoke always smells like anger and burnt-up dreams.

My Dad

Never trust anyone around you, my father tells me.

Not even the people I'm close with? I ask.

Especially not the people you're close with, he answers. They're the only people who can hurt you. Always choose yourself.

That wasn't his philosophy back when I was growing up. When I was younger, my dad used to always tell me that I should always treat everybody the way that I wanted to be treated. Sometimes, that meant lending my friend a pencil. Other times, it meant that I should give up my seat in the concert. But whatever it was in the moment, it was never avoidance. Never distance, never distrust and definitely never the selfishness behind always choosing yourself. I don't know if I'm mad at him. I think I'm just disappointed. Disappointed that when I've finally become the person he's always prided himself in being and taught me to be, he's changed to become unrecognizable. It makes me want to smash something. It also makes me want to ask questions.

Where does that leave me and my mama? What does family even mean? Are we our all, too, just disposable people he's decided to avoid because he's too afraid to trust? And finally, hopefully without crying, ask him whether that's the reason he found another family.

Love

What is love? Young adult books say love is a tumultuous ride of heartbreaks and possibility. My mama says love is company. My father says love is perseverance. But I don't think I know what love is because everyone loves so differently.

My Uncle Feng and my Aunt Ning fell in love in college. They got married in their twenties and built their place in the world hand in hand. I'd like to think that they loved each other. But my Uncle Feng and my Aunt Ning didn't last. They fought all the time. Fought over dishes, books, children, money and sometimes even a flower. But I guess at the end of the day it was never about the dishes, books, children, money or flower at all. It was about how they could never seem to get loving each other right. And it didn't mean they didn't love each other. There were always big gestures – big arguments followed with big apologies and big gifts and big words that all spelled out "I love you." Their love was splendid and their love was always in the air. It was so obvious to everyone else looking in. Yet my Aunt Ning always felt like my Uncle Feng didn't love her and vice versa. And that's the problem. It was never that they didn't love each other. Just that they didn't know how love each other the way they each needed to be loved. My Uncle Feng and Aunt Ning eventually went their separate ways.

My Uncle Feng got remarried three years later. This time, there was no honeymoon, no big gestures, no wedding that involved every family member of every generation. Yet it somehow didn't mean that he loved my new aunt any less. Their love was just quiet. The everyday-living-life kind of quiet. The they-found-peace-in-simply-being-okay-with-who-they-are kind of quiet. And that didn't mean they didn't argue. It's just meant that their arguments all got sat down, solved and resolved before bed. They never went to bed upset at each other. And the funny thing is, on book, they were so far from compatible. They shared no hobbies, no mutual friends, and even their taste in brownies was different. But they still made it work. And because this love was different from every love I'd known and seen growing up, I found myself constantly questioning if it was real at all. Is it really love without all the fancy confessions, intense emotions and pretty gifts? But I know their love is real, I know because it's been 10 years since they got married and they now have two kids and a dog. What is love actually supposed to look like? Are butterflies in your stomach actually love? Or is it supposed to look more like a stream of patience?

While I don't know the answer to all those questions, I'd like to think that the love between Feng and Ning was still real because that's what me and my mama are like. We argue about everything. We argue about where I put my shoes, the amount of conditioner I use, and how much soy sauce I put on my noodles. But we still love each other. And I guess I'd like to think that this type of love is real love because it's the only love I know.

Fruit Bowl

Everyone knows the joke about Asian parents and their fruit bowls. The gist is that, instead of apologizing, they would bring a bowl of fruits upstairs because "I'm sorry" burns the roof of their mouths like acid. I guess that holds true to some degree because until I was in 10th grade, I never heard the words "I'm sorry" come from my mother's mouth.

I'm sorry I couldn't keep my marriage out of your life, she said, I'm sorry. It's not your fault.

I guess she'd discovered the pressure from my aunts to fix things. That it was my fault — at least according to everyone else.

I guess I don't ever want to hear those words from her again. Her "I'm sorrys" carry a weight and responsibility that I am not ready to shoulder.

First Love Again

I don't like to call it a second love because I don't think I ever loved Leo, so I just call it a first love again every time I talk about her.

Natalie. Her name grips my gut in tension. I stare at the swoosh of her shoulder-length brown hair on the basketball court. Swish. Another hoop. I used to hate Natalie back in middle school when she was Olivia's best friend. I hated the way she gossiped. Woooaaaah. Another cheer. The way she so easily fit in. Bam. Another high five. And mostly the way that we're both Asian American students but she somehow just seems that much more likable than me. Thunk – another lay-up.

I don't know. I only know that the more I stare at her brown eyes, the more I find myself laughing. They hold a warmth so brilliant it can melt any ice into a summer's breeze. But I hate myself when I stare at her. I hate the brows that soften the moment my eyes land on her. Hate the hands that can't seem to keep her out of my sketchbook. Hate the mouth that instantly loses all of its words when Natalie asks a question. Why can't I get her off my mind?

She's just pretty. She's just smart. She just can't shut up. You just want to fit in. You just want to be like her. That must be why she's always on my mind. That must be why I can't seem to have a moment of peace to myself without wondering what her lips might taste like.

But how long can I really lie to myself when the answers are right there?

This is the first time I've liked a girl and I'm scared. Scared because I don't want to be yet another weird-hair-colored-emo-smokey-eyed lesbian. Scared because I've just stepped a whole foot out of line. Scared because even though I've been called every name in my life, I'm lost. I don't have a guide on how to be gay and Asian.

Camila and Natalie

What do you mean that you like Natalie? You're not supposed to like Natalie! Is that why you refused to go on a double date with Jordan and me? Hold on, hold on. Screw that. Did you ever have a crush on me? Camila's demanding voice echoes. Suddenly, I would like to run out of the English classroom.

Instead, I sit still, head spinning as I take another sip of my Arizona raspberry tea. I savor the sweet taste on my tongue before I let myself take on her barrage of questions. *Did you ever have a crush on me?* No, I never did. But I don't know how to tell Camila. I don't know because this moment reminds me of one of those coming-out movies. It's always this question that destroys the friendship. I mean, if you look at it, there are no right answers – if I tell the truth, Camila will be offended, and if I lie, we'll never talk again. I take another sip of my raspberry tea and weigh my options. I'd rather be honest with her, I guess.

No, I say.

Am I not attractive? she follows up.

No, you are. You're just not my type or something, I say.

You're blushing! she says.

I'm not but I don't bother to correct her. It's the fact that we've spent every minute of the last year together and she knows nothing about me. So much nothing that she can't even tell I'm being honest right now. I close my eyes and let her think whatever because I don't want to be friends with Camila anymore.

Asian Love

No one in Uncle John's family really understands what he gives up every day for them. They see him as just a pestering old man who does the unnecessary every day. They understand to be grateful but not what they should be grateful for. But I know. I know that the thing to thank him for isn't the barbecue he prepared or the money he provides when he goes to work. It's the care behind every action and how he pulls and pulls and pulls every possible burden on top of himself. Asian heritage is not knowing how to love.

Uncle John loves his family a lot. I know because I can tell. I can tell from the way he shuts his mouth and forces himself to work, from the way he blames himself for every problem, from the way he talks about his daughter. Take care of Melody for me Nicole, will you? Make sure she doesn't do stupid things. She's not as mature as you. She's not as strong as you. Life hasn't hit her yet and I don't want it to.

Melody understands a different hell from mine. In hers, people are starving and struggling and sprinting together towards the light of education and money. In my hell, people are rich. They're full of lies and greed and hidden meanings lurk in their words, ready to strike. In my world, there isn't a light, just to use or be used, and money is the only goal in life. The up and the down. That's what I like to call these two different hells.

Uncle John and I live in the same hell. Every grown-up I know, every child I know, every person struggling in the middle and upper classes trying to define where they want to be on this social ladder – we all end up in this hell eventually. Uncle John fights in this hell alone so no one in his family has to. That's the way he loves.

When I was young, I was similar to Melody as well. I never thought twice about loving or trusting. I cared for everyone's story, stranger or not, and lent a hand whenever I could. But life forces people to grow up. I can't help everyone and I don't have ears to listen to every story. I'm much more cautious of my feathers now because even if I know I can help, I also know that I'm not always in a position to give. I just want to live my life the way I do with no expectations of glorious, good deeds.

I wish I had an Uncle John in my family because I wish there was someone protecting me when I was growing up. I wish I was as excited as Melody looking forward to the outside world.

Pretty

You can call me obsessed with being pretty because I am. Having spent so long as a green leaf, I was done, I was tired of being ignored. Nowadays, I wake up 30 minutes earlier every morning to do my makeup. I get to sleep an hour later so I can do my skin care. I've learnt to perfectly manage all my outfits, aesthetics and even attitude to become the person I want to be. I knew I was no longer the ugly duckling of a friend anymore when Camila and I stopped talking. I am my own flower.

But Uncle John's daughter is much prettier than me. Pretty in the way that she's happy with who she is and pretty in the way she cares about the people around her. I've spent my entire life trying to be pretty. And I am. I'm magazine-picture-perfect-girl pretty. Walking-the-streets-and-get-asked-for-your-number pretty. But I'm not as pretty as she is. Not in the same way, at least.

We're sitting on an airplane together flying to Minnesota and I have my head buried in my pillow, trying desperately to shut voices out while Melody has her head buried in her iPad, trying to sketch the old lady next to her. Yolanda, she says, you're such an interesting person. Yolanda, what was life like in Puerto Rico like? Yolanda, Yolanda, Yolanda. The seats next to me are a sea of giggles.

I've learned all my life how to talk to people in the up while Melody's has become the voice of the down. Pampered, bratty, confused. I'm unrecognizable. Being pretty and stupid is my best bet in the middle and upper classes and I hate myself for it, but I choose to anyway. I choose to because I want to get things done. I need to get things done. Every word I say, every painting I paint, every move I make, I get things done. Always have a goal in mind, my father says. Always know how you're going to get there. I guess that's the thing: when every action is motivated, I begin to forget how to do the whole organic socialization thing. And I guess that's what makes Melody so pretty. Pretty in the way that she cares about everyone. Pretty in the way that she actually connects with people. Words are her bridges to love and my weapons to wield. But I guess that's what I had to sacrifice to get things done.

It's only in moments like this when I'm staring out an airplane window, looking at the horizon, wondering what pretty looks like that I feel free. I'm not really talkative by nature. Or maybe I was when I was younger, but in general, I don't really like talking. I prefer silence. Yet nowadays, I'm the most talkative person I know, comfortable in her ability to wield language as a weapon. But whenever I can, I still find myself silent. No longer silent in rebellion but silent in peace and relief.

Naïveté is very pretty.

Breaking Up

We should talk, Mason messages.

My smart mouth runs dry. I don't want to talk to him. I don't want to have face the emotional consequences of ignoring him for the last week. I don't want to break up. Not yet. Not until we're both perfectly over each other. I stare at the breakup script I wrote a week ago. How am I supposed to just read this thing out loud? How can we just both move on after telling each other we cared for the last three months?

Okay, I type, call me whenever.

My entire body is fluttering and I can feel my heart echo in her empty cell. It's warm. I just showered. I'm shivering. My hands can't hold still. Ten minutes pass and I hear nothing from him.

Call me first, Mason messages again. Call me first for once.

I pretend not to let his passive aggressiveness get to me. Ow. I squeeze my thigh too hard. I slowly dial his 10 digits into my phone. Am I going to have to change his contact? I don't want to block him. What about the friendship we had before? I don't know.

I dial the number. Uncertainty is my worst enemy. I don't know how to feel and I'm having a hard time trying to keep my tea down. The loss of someone or something always comes so fast, so real, and I am not ready. No, not when I've always felt like I was in control. I like being in control. And ridiculously, in the spur of this moment, watching the dial ring, I don't even know if he will pick up.

Many like to describe the passing of time with each tick of the clock, or with each grain of sand or droplet of water that slips past and through their fingertips. I prefer it as watching a train crash in slow motion. And the dread of watching it happen. The despair in knowing what will come but feeling powerless to put it to a halt. The future predicts itself. So what's the stress?

Anxiety. That's the word. I turn up my music one more notch; it's burning my ears. I pick up. His voice rings cold in my mind. Silence. I close my eyes and try to think. I find myself rambling. I speak a gibberish that he understands but I don't. Are they excuses? Are they truths that I have even lied to myself about? I don't know.

We don't end up blocking each other but I don't talk to him either. Mason and I aren't really exes. We're best friends in past tense.

Wish

Her name is Wish. Well, the Chinese character of her surname means wish and that's just what I've been calling her. It's ironic because the first piece I wrote about coming out back in eighth grade is titled *Want*. Back then, I wanted Spotify Premium and no more necklaces in my life. And now I guess Spotify Premium has elevated to new clothes and want into wish.

Wish is the first girl that makes me want to break rules. She makes me want to skip class and get boba. For months, she has made me want to march into my house and tell Mama that I like to kiss girls. She makes me want to let the whole world know that she's mine. But I know I can't. I can't because liking girls is the nudge that pushes me across the Last Asian Threshold. I can't because I know what Mama will say. Not that she hates me or wants me to go to hell but that I'm just a little confused and time will sort things out. I know she won't force us apart. She'll just cry alone, praying that I can be normal, and hoping to god that I haven't left her the way my father did. Mama won't even say a word to make me upset, she'll just silently walk away and I'll have to live, kissing Wish, knowing the fact that Mama doesn't forgive me. I can't. Mama is the only family I have left so I can't. I lie to her even though it's not true.

"I'm sorry, Wish. I think I lost feelings and maybe we're better off as friends anyway."

The Yi in Hongyi

伊 stands for "a pretty girl" in Chinese, my father always told me.

It means you'll grow up to be independent, unique and beautiful, my mama would add on.

And from the Chinese tradition of synthesizing a nickname from the last character of your name, I became known as 伊伊. I liked it. I've always liked being called 伊伊 because it made me feel pretty, girly, yet strong.

But not even my Chinese teachers seemed to be able to get the character quite right. Every time a report card would come, somewhere, someone definitely spelt my name as 依依 instead. And although they are pronounced the same, 伊 and 依 mean largely different things. While my name stands for independence and beauty, 依, the more common and more effeminate counterpart means to depend on, to obey, and to comply with. I hate it when people use the wrong form of "yi" when they refer to me. I don't like to feel weak.

I'm sitting on the edge of my bed alone in the house on my 18th birthday when my father messages me. He and I don't talk a lot nowadays, either because he's too busy for me or because I pretend like I'm too busy for him. But I look at the message today anyway because I want to know what he has to say. Apparently, he's done some writing about me for my college counselors to brainstorm personal statements from and wants me to read it over. I'm immediately disappointed. In his fourth sentence and the only time he uses my name in the entire selection of 13k words, he has used the wrong form of "yi."

I know I always say that I don't care about whether my father knows me. Yet before I can even read the sentence twice, my eyes are already watering and I'm chewing on my lips. He has used the wrong form of yi. You'd think that the person who named me would know how to spell their own child's name correctly, right? You'd think that in 13k words he would refer to my name more than once, right? But no, I'm simply referred to as "the child" and 依依 in his writing. But I guess it doesn't matter anyway because people only know me as Nicole.

Gay Christmas Trees

It's been a year now and I'm finally fine with being gay. It's not that bad. I can now successfully walk around the school proudly hitting on girls. But that's the problem. I'm proud of being bisexual, but I don't like pride. I mean, the whole concept of decorating oneself ostentatiously like a gay Christmas tree feels diminishing. Why would you want your whole identity to hang upon one thing? I'd like to think I have plenty of accomplishments of my own that I should be proud of first. Like hey, I think of myself as a Devin scientist before being a gay guy. Or that I'm a writer before I'm bisexual.

Ironically, in the next school production, I was cast as the most stereotypical lesbian known to man. Diane had pink closely cropped hair, Blundstone boots, red and black flannels, and wore a white tank top. They might as well have carved G-A-Y into her forehead.

That couldn't have been necessary, I say, complaining to my director.

Well Nicole, my director sighs, you have to realize that however the character might be depicted, it doesn't make her more or less gay than any other gay character.

Yeah exactly, I protest, so why does she have to wear a flannel and boots? You know, since her sexuality isn't defined by visual signifiers.

My director sighs again.

We spend the next month creating a "fuller image": her favorite color is pink, her favorite cartoon is *SpongeBob*, her favorite tea is between chai and matcha, her favorite season is autumn, and she goes salsa dancing every Saturday. By the production, Diane was more than her overt gayness. I guess that's when I started reflecting: regardless of people and their relationship to stereotypes, they, at heart, are still individuals.

Coming Out

I came out later that year. The funny thing is the first person I came out to was my dad. I guess I just felt like coming out for the first time should be in front of people close to you – people close like family. Ironically, my dad and I aren't close at all. But I guess that's also the reason I was comfortable coming out to him. I don't know, I guess it just worked out in my head that since we weren't close, I wouldn't have to be responsible for his emotions and that if there was any negative feedback, I could simply ignore it. His opinions of me mean nothing. I guess that's also why I haven't come out to my mama – because I'd be terrified if it made her love me any less.

Boyfriend

Guys after Mason come and go. It's almost like the world was playing some unanimous prank on me where nobody found me attractive for the first 17 years of my life and then suddenly boom, a switch clicked and I was a hot commodity. I don't know what changed. Maybe because I got prettier, maybe because I became more confident. Maybe because I'm more unapologetic.

My mama doesn't like it when I date around, so I don't tell her about the guys that come and go. Not the ones that have cheated, not the ones that have loved me. And never the ones that don't make it past the first date.

Don't let guys use you for your body, she says.

Don't let guys break your heart, she says.

Don't find the people who can't actually love you, she says.

But we're in high school. We're 18 and just teenagers. We're still so young and lost. And I just laugh and tell her no guys like me because none of it matters anyway. All this time wasted and I'm just subconsciously looking for a shadow of my dad in every person I talk to. The days of my childhood when I wanted to be with someone like my dad are long gone. None of it matters anyway.

The Beauty of Gray

Back in China, I started my art portfolio over the summer. Hours and hours of self-portraits dry into clumps of paint on my wooden palette. I watch the colors swish and mix, splashing different versions of myself onto canvas.

What's your favorite color? I asked my art teacher when I was back in China.

Gray, she said, I like the color gray. In the first hour of painting, the paint dries pink, purple, yellow, blue, brown. In the second hour of painting, the paint dries muted purple, muted green, muted orange, and brown. In the fifth hour of painting, the paint dries gray purple, gray green, gray orange and gray. By the 30th hour of painting, every original color dries gray. Different shades maybe, but always gray.

Can we clear the palette again? I ask my art teacher.

Well Nicole, you know, you'll have to eventually learn how to work with gray, you know.

I hate gray, I say, it's such an ugly mix of everything.

No, no, she says, it's the most beautiful color of all. After all, everything in life ends up being gray, just like your palette. You might have a brilliant red or blue or green to start with, but eventually, with enough mixing, time and growth, everything turns into gray.

We keep painting for another 30 hours. Maybe gray isn't that bad. Maybe gray isn't insecure. Maybe gray is just being okay with being a little bit of everything. Maybe gray is good enough.

Confrontations

You have a mistress, don't you? I say. I am surprisingly calm when the words fall out of my mouth. Breathe in, breathe out.

Your half-brother is two, my dad replies.

I stare down at the sizzling steak on my plate. It's garnished perfectly with a light touch of rosemary and thyme. I take a deep breath in, letting the sweet scent of butter and wasted gold saturate my lungs and nod. I don't want to look my dad in the eyes. Instead, I take a sip from my wine glass. The bittersweet taste washes over my mouth and I wince.

I've been drinking alcohol since I landed in China. And frankly, I hate it. I like neither the red-hot Chinese spirits that send fireworks down my throat nor the spikey bitterness of red wine that tickles my chest funny. I just drink because it makes me seem mature. That's the only way my dad will be able to see me as an equal. I'm so desperate for him to stop keeping me in the dark that I forget I'm still just a kid.

I take another sip of the wine and cough. I'm not sure if I'm crying from the alcohol or what he's said.

I'm sorry I wasn't a good father to you, he says, I would just like to be more present in your brother's childhood. I'm sorry. That's why I haven't visited.

I nod. We've been both so equally absent in each other's lives that we're barely even strangers by this point. And who am I to judge him? I have no standing in his life to state an opinion or stake an accusation. We are simply strangers related by blood. I nod again.

Hero

Who is your hero?

Growing up, my answer was something generic like Lei Feng or my dad. I don't know, I guess I just never really put any thought to it. The idea of having a hero is so... heroic. You know, like you're living life with a clear trail to follow. And so, these easy, common answers that never prompted any follow-up questions became my opt-out choice. Yet I find that, as I slowly settle into my last high school, an initially ironic kind of answer begins to surface.

My hero is named Makoto. Makoto is an emo, frustrated little ball of energy that I stumbled upon playing video games. Never good at communicating but always living life with a critical eye, he guides me through who I think I need to be.

No one gives a flying crap about what you wear, he'll say.

Get up here and grab lunch; you're not skipping today, he'll say.

I don't know what I'm doing either, okay?? he'll say.

Through this series of complaining, fighting, struggling and trying to make better decisions together, Makoto found me a home. Some will say he was my key to becoming a social reject. I say that he's my hero.

I call him my hero because he isn't some sort of savior. I'm not some lost little girl stuck in a ditch and he's not a ray of sunshine that pulled me out of it. In fact, he's probably quite the opposite. I call him my hero because he's a wakeup call. He's stable, consistent, an unironic-yet-somehow-not-book-smart-nerd, and at the core, just himself. Makoto lives content with just who he is and that's what makes him heroic.

And I guess that's also why he's strong. Strong in the sense that his strength isn't inspired by brilliance or trauma but because he's accepting of everyone and everything. Including himself. Don't get me wrong, that's not to say he doesn't judge. In truth, he's probably one of the most opinionated people I know. And trust me, in his honest, straightforward nature, his thoughts will find you, one way or another. But I guess that's the way he loves and that's the way I need to be loved. Makoto is the hopeful yet pessimistic twist of reality everyone needs in their life.

Whenever I get stuck in life, Makoto pushes me. That's how he loves me. By making me look my dumb decisions in the eye. By sticking with me no matter how stupid they sound. Makoto makes me keep digging until I'm where I want to be.

Kat, you don't have to find a light to be happy, he'll say, you can be your own light. You don't have to look for more. You're enough.

And that is good enough.

Proud and Loud

My view on pride solidified a change when I blew up at my cousin for supporting China's new laws banning all LGBTQ+ forums in school.

You can't just not let people express themselves, I exclaim.

They are giving *kids* the *wrong* ideas! he retorts.

No they're not, I defend. They simply give *gay kids* a *platform* *t*o feel *supported.*

As someone who never sought to loudly advocate for the pride of being gay, I found myself arguing most vociferously. In that moment, I wanted everyone there to know that I was gay, proud and not afraid to defend my rights. *I* was that gay kid who needed a forum like that. And I refuse to let it be taken away from anyone else.

And then it hit me. Back in the U.S., in the comfort of acceptance, it is easy to call these events anachronistic or silly, but in places where homosexuality is oppressed, it becomes important to see proud proclamations of gayness and protests of injustice.

For the second time ever, I attended pride this summer. Although I still wasn't a dash of rainbow like Devin, I brought markers of my own bisexuality – rainbow pins that I passed out; humble, proud and gay, just like me.

Home

My mama says that we're selling the house when I graduate. I don't offer any other opinion. It's not like I can expect her to stay in America and take care of a damn house after I'm off to college. I've already kept so many years of her life hostage and we both know that an old house is a feisty waste of time. But still, knowing that we are going to sell the house tugs at my gut in the wrong way. House. House. House. This inanimate dwelling of a residence could have maybe been considered a house six years ago when we first moved in. But after all these years? These six long years of decorations, erosions of living and even just feeding the koi fish in the pond... I would rather call it a home. I've never had a home before this and I really didn't want to let go. Who knows when I'll find a home again?

What's the difference between a house and a home? I ponder. I guess it's just the memories. I guess it's the feelings and sentiments. These memories, feelings, sentiments, good or bad, leave forever imprints. That's what makes something a home.

Memories overshadow every inch of this house. An argument in the living room. A first kiss on the third floor. A pillow fight with Andrea in the bedroom. A breakdown while playing piano. *I* have filled every inch of this house. It's my home.

I wonder what happens when we finally sell the house. Am I homeless again? When I was younger, I used to consider my mama my home. Wherever she went I called home. But the start of college marks a new stage of my life where she won't be around anymore. And in terms of actual dwellings? Well, I can't go back to China – I already can't bear facing all the relatives and I just know I won't be able to meet my dad's new family like it's nothing. I'm not strong enough. I guess I will just have to settle in America. Start something new and leave everything behind. But here, I'm alone. Alone in my exploration and even lonelier in my company. I guess from now on I can only call myself "home."

Nicole

I go by Nicole nowadays. I guess Katarina just lost touch as I slowly grew up – too sharp, too loud, too competitive. I think I like the idea of Nicole. Somehow, somewhere, sometime, she's grown out of the suburban housewife and, in her self-awareness and vulnerability, has grown into the responsible leader people in her life need her to be.

My writing is gentler nowadays. I tend to think of my work less as a mess and bloodshed of rage and hate. I guess James Baldwin's *Notes of a Native Son* changed my mind. It changed my mind because I didn't want to grow up to be like his father, or my father, or anyone's enraged father. I didn't want to be marked by hatred. I didn't want to be crushed by anger. I want to be strong with love. Strong, subtle, silent. The way his uncle was, the way my mother is.

I stopped worrying about my dad and focused more on my mother when I came back home from China. I came out to her with a slam poem a few months ago. We sat in the kitchen, Jay Chow in the background, splitting a bowl of black sesame paste as I translated my writing line by line for her.

I just don't want your life to be harder than it is, she said. I nodded. Love is acceptance.

Your father and I got a divorce, she said. I nodded. Love is letting go.

I love you, she said. I nodded again. Love is perseverance and we both had a lot more work to do.

I love you, I whispered back.

ABOUT THE AUTHOR

Nicole is an 18-year-old aspiring author. In this book, she seeks to address issues of cultural shock through the Chinese-American immigrant perspective via vignettes. As a child, Nicole constantly struggled with the different impacts of distinct cultures as she moved across states and continents. As a writer, she is motivated by her experiences and uses storytelling to fuel her passions of introspection, arts, and communication. Her stories, through their diverse perspectives, seek to create a more inclusive society.

Made in the USA
Middletown, DE
28 July 2023